THE
ZOO WHEEL
OF
KNOWLEDGE

HENRI COLE

*T*HE
ZOO WHEEL
O F
KNOWLEDGE

ALFRED A KNOPF

New York   1989

ACKNOWLEDGMENTS : The author wishes to record his thanks to editors of the following publications, where poems, often in different form, were originally published:

ANTAEUS: "Ascension on Fire Island"
THE ATLANTIC: "The Annulment"
BOULEVARD: "O," "Lines on Seeing the First Color Photograph of Planet Mars"
COLUMBIA: A MAGAZINE OF POETRY & PROSE: "The Best Man"
THE GETTYSBURG REVIEW: "Tuxedo," "The Zoo Wheel of Knowledge"
THE NEW YORKER: "Boy's Life"
ONTARIO REVIEW: "American Girl"
THE PARIS REVIEW: "West Point Remembered," "Vanessa"
POETRY: "Cape Cod Elegy," "A Half-Life"
SOUTHWEST REVIEW: "Papilloma," "Caesar"
THE WILLIAM AND MARY REVIEW: "Three Look at One Another"
THE YALE REVIEW: "St. Stephen's Day with the Griffins," "Lost in Venice"

The author also wishes to record his thanks to the Corporation of Yaddo, for providing an ideal setting in which part of this collection was written, and to the New York Foundation for the Arts, for providing financial support during this book's completion.

Library of Congress Cataloging-in-Publication Data

Cole, Henri.
    The zoo wheel of knowledge / Henri Cole. — 1st ed.
        p.   cm.
    ISBN 0–394–58066–4
    ISBN 0–679–72594–6 (pbk.)
    I. Title.
PS3553.04725Z39   1989
811'.54—dc20   89–45307
                                                    CIP

To my sisters,
Patricia and Suzanne,
and to
Gardner,
a sister in every way

Contents

CONTENTS

viii

THE
ZOO WHEEL
OF
KNOWLEDGE

Advent

Driving rainfall. The nation a sniffling white
rabbit plunged in its hutch. Stew in the oven
and a softly radiant glow from the den
unlock our children's hearts. In one's dilated

pupil, the strawberry-blue body, slim
on its stalk with rain-tossed hair, shines against
the blankness everywhere, lucent as Mother's mending
needles speared with a sigh in tiger skin.

I

A Half-Life

There is no sun today,
save the finch's yellow breast,
and the world seems faultless in spite of it.
Across the sound, a continuous
ectoplasm of gray,
a ferry slits the deep waters,

bumping our tiny motorboats
against their pier.
The day ends like any day,
with its hour of human change
lifting even the choleric heart.
If living in someone else's dream

makes us soft, then I am so,
spilling out from the lungs
like green phlegm of spring.
My friend resting on the daybed
fills his heart with memory,
as July's faithful swallows

weave figure-eights above him,
vaulting with pointed wings and forked tails
for the ripe cherries he tosses them,
then ascending in a frolic
of fanned umbrella-feathers
to thread a far, airy steeple.

To my mind, the cherries form an endless
necklacelike cortex rising out
of my friend's brain, the swallows
unravelling the cerebellum's pink cord.
In remission six months, his
body novocained and fallow,

he trembles, threadbare, as the birds unwheel him.
The early evening's furnace casts
us both in a shimmering sweat.
In a wisp Gabriel might appear to us,
as to Mary, announcing a sweet
miracle. But there is none.

The lilies pack in their trumpets,
our nesting dove nuzzles her eggs,
and chameleons color their skin with dusk.
A half-life can be deepened by the whole,
sending out signals of a sixth sense,
as if the unabashed, youthful eye

sees clearest to the other side.
A lemon slice spirals in the icy tea,
a final crystal pulse of sun reappears,
and a newer infinite sight
takes hold of us like the jet of color
at the end of winter. Has it begun:

the strange electric vision of the dying?
Give me your hand, friend.
Come see the travellers arrive.
Beneath the lazy, bankrupt sky,
theirs is a world of joy trancing
even the gulls above the silver ferry.

The Annulment

for my nephew

After a time, because they could not love
one another as they could others,
what became of you recalled my infant brother,
lost in Limbo, his breath elusive
as crib death, waiting in a field for the world's end.
So when the Church unleashed them from their hearts,
undoing the words that were forever, through the dark
glass there was nothing but her earrings golden
in the moonlight and the torque of his neck as he
raced the motor of their Triumph. Though they
transgressed and wandered incalculably,
you rose out of them, lacquered from your journey
and muttering vowels like all the lost children,
souls breathed forth, sitting up in their graves to sing.

Saint Stephen's Day with the Griffins

for Janet and Christopher

Half-eagle, half-lion, the fabulous
    animal struts, saber-clawed but saintly,
a candlewicked ornament dangling
from our rickety sugar pine. Butternut

    pudding in our bellies. His reindeer
        and sleigh hurried here and gone—thank God
    for us childless folks. Almost: the lovelocked
Griffins on the sofa, sockfooted, hearing

    gas and a kiddy heart in her tummy—
        a life more imaginary than real,
    though one is dazzled by gold that fills
this egg unbroken. We feed her crumpets

    and listen again: The lamb's a hungry
        bugger, even snug from earth's
    imponderable fury. Tomorrow, in a spurt
by jet I'm home. Clumsy as a puppy

    I'll scale the flightstairs into the nosecone,
        luggage banging at my sides, enter the egg-
    shaped cabin and await the infrared
climb toward space. Tell me one

    thing true? If I could count the way
        things slip from us: Mother's fur gloves,
    Sunday's benediction, the dead gone before us,
love's rambler on the prairie—all displaced

as we buckle in our shuttle,
     jetbound on a screaming runway,
     gravity pulling at us castaways,
more mammal than bird, subtle

     leg-weary griffins made manifest,
          arrowing towards home. How do we
     ignore it: the attenuated being
of our age, the bittersweet collapse

     of dominoes mooned around our pine?
          Withered with hatred from his quarter,
     Saint Stephen even at death rolled mercifully over
in high holiness. Sonless, wifeless, nine

     thousand feet from land, I roll the lozenge
          on my tongue, youthful habit for ache
     of any kind, parting a survivor (Wait!),
love rescuing me from the fringe.

The Best Man

As after a long rowing match, the crew
collapsed forward upon its oars, we taxi
over the Georgian meadow and ascend,
nose tipped earthward like the Concorde,
into the holy peace of aerospace
and the sonic hum of our Cessna
Atlantis express. My neighbor, her legs crossed
beneath a white sailor skirt, peruses *Money*,
turning each page with a lick and snap of her index;
her skin is bronzed and we sit together
in its scent of sweet petals
as the glittering silt of Savannah uncoils beneath us
in reptilian serenity across a forest
of twigs where my brother's bridal awaits me.
Spark of sunlight on the ovalpane,
mistiness of cumulus, our Jetstreamer
transforms into an airborne chapel, the Trinity—
that rarest of all blends, efficient
and sympathetic—at the cockpit
administering its indissoluble sacrament
to my brother, clean-lived and provident,
and his bride Helen (believe it!), whose
parsley crown, symbol of chastity,
is fresh as her mother's wedding dress
chilled for a quarter century
and illumined like a chandelier
for this ancestral union.
The sun gleams golden in my eyes,
the hour reversing further in its blaze
to a precommunion moment, my brother
and I bleached clean from morning laps
(I'd seen him scissoring through the blue oasis
outsmoothed in the meters ahead of us,

his white throat swanlike and curved as a woman's),
smart in our morning suits, ascot and tails
painting us more alike than real.
Which one is me? Reborn in the tilt of past
things told or future made existent, I am
witness, and on this consummate occasion, groomsman,
clean from the shore of irreconcilable dreams,
of man separate, eternally unwedded,
yet pirouetting in separateness:
a small cross to carry in such a long
calvary of a life! Which one am I?
In a silver-sequined jet whispering mid-air,
I sit at the apex of three glistening tailfins,
a trillion trees feathering towards us,
a Bible-belt debutante dozing beside me
into the rich, delta incubus of sleep.
A holy calm like the peace of God
passing all understanding drops its curtain
upon us. Hosannas rise from the sutra
of plane din, from the pressurized
chamber's vibrant Ommmmmmm
of penetrating high-altitudinal space.
Godspeed, brother and sister. Swim with the armor
of arctic fish. As the hour's quarters
dong past, dandle the axis of your devotion,
learn the million nuances of your hearts.
As the year's faces metamorphose before you,
and Time soaks the fire between you
and you emerge dripping from the sea, golden
with the voltage of Life, your palms
like bronze gongs still clasped, know that melancholy,
that meanness (or even *Money!*)—
the spidery scalpels of marriage,
a grave when you stand at their center—
fade quickly into the playful, sweet sting
of the middle-aged, then the snowy Pleistocene of December:

Old-fashion advice—half of me wishes to do this
with you; the other half, the baby as odd-shaped
as an octopus, says, *Be well. Bring me a bee
from Paradise. Think a little, dream a lot!
This sacrament is an impractical knot,
but you'll undo its mischievous divinities.*
In my mid-air chapel, a dome of blue
sky overhead, your happiness is perpetual,
and our Cessna, like a chariot, carries you
toward something infinite and irresistible.

American Girl

On the beachroad
to the Paradise Discotheque,

my friend, sunbaked and lean as a birch,
and I tightrope the seawall, the surf's

uproar of foam spraying us
as we wander farther from home.

Gone now the seasonal crowd
after twelve weeks South,

fleeing in their battered taxis
to the island airstrip,

its moonstruck macadam glinting
like a purple pass to civilization.

We're all that's left.
And the ocean, spouting

scornful swallowtails of sea.
When my friend hooks a razor of beachglass

in her heel, we sit on a slab
of rock and inspect the bleeding zigzag.

The white flood of headlights
framing us in dreamlike

blur, her foot lies in my hand a slipper.
Sweet as Icarus, a young boy held her

the night before,
the Paradise's marble dance floor

reflecting them in its pink fibrous sky.
This morning all was changed: The hot-bright

strobes that circled them as if a beacon
from God's eye, bold as the sun,

went black, black as opium's
blinding delirium,

as heaven on orbiting earth,
and man and braying beast on the far

skyline . . . And when that eye opened,
stubborn Icarus had flown.

Like the ocean rising, dragging itself
from alluvial embrace, the carnal

mind lifts itself unacquiescent.
Each dizzying car that passes

weaves another thread of tapestry—
Can she see its otherworldly

self? Earrings jingling, a dozen
silver bracelets singing on her wrists,

marrow roaring in her spine:
Of course! she sighs. What choice but to arrest it?

Her thin heel rinsed gently in the sea
and snugly kerchiefed, her sandals strapped, we

stand there alone a moment
before turning home,

lunar-bright and sea-changed,
into the black mountain-flame.

West Point Remembered

Such is the way with monumental things:
to make us see and wonder.
The unreserved calm of the place
made us marvel at the world's problems.
Across the post office lawn
cadets gathered in twos and threes,
each man with trousers pressed
and six gilded buttons riveted
in a field of grey. They greeted each
other with perfect Victorian courtesy,
and one with his head cocked in daydream,
cap pushed back at a boyish slant,
a yellow letter unfolded and waving
in his hand, asked himself,
as any one of us might,
"What do the words mean?"
The liquid tattoos of blue ink
ran across his page, a river
of pewter-bright clarity,
yet clarifying only the silence
he felt as he looked past us
toward the real river, a fishy, neglected,
luminous streak of blue, gull-raked,
and running wide as the Hudson's base.
Not one of us, as I recall, could deny
the difficult note he heard.
To listen more than one speaks
is a gift despite its pinch of misery,
and what the cadet from his citadel
heard comes seldom in a life.
His nation like a Parthenon
seemed risen where even the miracle
of scruffy house-wrens find their lungs

fire-branded by the thin air.
And all afterwards that color-peak weekend,
our windshield carried with it
a dim sepia print of this scene
as though rendering the letter's dispatch.
A hunk of scarlet foliage
electrified all around us
as we coasted down the new mown meadow
to spend the day cheering
a corps of plebes in their pickup scrimmage,
our thermos filling us
with its creamy, sedating gold
as the ageless players
clipped one another like silver knives
with such force and skill it seemed they
cut loose the very detritus of our lives.

The Roosevelt Spa

Down the cool, cool corridors
of the Roosevelt, named for our
big-game-hunting statesman, there are
rooms for each of us small

enough to keep a canary in.
Father and son, still dreamy
from the racetrack, take the first pair.
Mine's the one with the weary

philodendron, its tub ivory
as a christening font till Eddie
(his name embroidered on his chest),
all in white with averted eyes,

fills it nearly to my head.
The spring is hot and emerald green
and bubbles beneath me like champagne.
My arms and legs lighten

and lighten exactly as in space.
"Remember Velvet Fog in the eighth race?"
someone somewhere says as I
flood the world with a fetal dive.

Underneath only the soft purr
of air rises up, up
through the saline, glaucous bath,
up from the center of earth.

The winter I was nine
Father took me swimming
at the Pentagon. Bald and pink-
faced, ears in an upsweep,

even the grim Colonels swam naked
in the steamy natatorium.
That vision of man released
from power—submerged in aquamarine,

his dogged mind, a silver cabbage,
adrift as if on the sea, his limbs
translucent as a gecko's,
splashing in the blue lamplight,

his eyes goggled like a fly's
skimming the surface—fired
memory of a world
faraway as placental gold

of the birth canal. My heart
expanded in its cage of ribs,
darting like the soldier's helmeted
intellect, and the future stretched

its sapphire shore before me, an oracle
beheld in the ribbon of blue water
fanning in giant, radial
corollas. It was poolside, there

through youth, that the skewed, unimpeded
passage of history, foaming
like an underworld, came to me:
From breech birth to coins-on-the-eyes,

only an endless whoosh of wind,
crystal as spring water, would whirl
us into zones of what we become
toward ineluctable rest-in-peace—

so when Eddie comes back and helps me up
from the cures as if from a crib and wraps
me in a hot sheet, I feel baffled
and hungry and desert-struck.

A Sacred Heart

When I was a boy and bone-dry
with Christ, chastity was no
hallmark of a libertine. Only
the unbitten strayed. My

head was swamped with liturgy:
"If good spirits will not live
where there is dirt and there is
no dirt in Heaven, then that is where we

shall live, entering first for Holy
sanctuary, honoring it with chastity
and ravenously awaiting God"—
Unable to draw breath, my crown

of curls "ungodly," though free
(to me!) as Jesus's rain-swept mound,
I tasted first our joyless church.
Here is Christ, the scripture said,

Father Bradigan's green lizard specs
lowered at me. *Let Him have your heart,*
He'll give you immortality instead.
So I saved my soul, unharmed

by mortal sin, carrying Him
inside me till I was seven,
papal age of reason,
groomed for Communion

when congregates, save me, gave Him
their stone-faced grief. My dazed thoughts
were an arsenal that Pentecost,
my stomach empty for Jesus,

as Father's sweet tenor and Air
Force clippers poised at my nape:
"All set?" A bedsheet cape
caught angel wings of hair

descending from my
barbered crown. All the good angels
seemed to sail away from me,
a failed soldier of Christ,

so I needled with my wit:
How many angels fit
on the head of a new pin?
No answer came, till Father winked:

The purest, bodiless spirits,
as many as you want, Son.
Then the Judas in me rose up again,
seeking a trip

in the pious web: If I
plunged from a perilous
cliff in a perfect swan dive,
where would my personality go,

falling fourteen stories, lost
in a swirling chasm below?
Would it rise above the undertow
or snap shut in death's hatbox?

Looking the devilish thought
clear in my eye, an electrical
storm of hairline retinal
veins wavered across my father's

hazel eyes. Touching the boy
at his core, it seized him
like a crocodile, as coy
a riddle as any pulpit wisdom.

High on my yellow kitchen stool,
I, the perilous diver, held his eye.
Not dreamily as I might
the band of tourists fancied

across the gorge, their salt-rimmed
tequila swirling in tumblers
as they cheered the beautiful divers
on, but bold as a Christian

icon, a sad Hollywood Christ
exalted, taking our breath
like a crucifix, like the fiery
swan diver sporting a zesty

red cape and a blazing torch
in each hand, his votive candle
snuffed out at sixty miles an hour
as he hits the choppy surf.

Not a trace of scorn flickered
in his eyes as Father
snapped the sheet from my neck
and billowed it like a spinnaker,

shaking loose the feathery
ambiguity of my hair.
And I hopped down, ironed
for adventure.

That day the chalice rose and fell,
the tasteless wafer eaten.
Over and over, advanced and retreated
in time, it leaves only a veiled

sequence of opened mouths
risen toward the sky,
and a thick runner of tongue
interconnected by the child

in each of us kicking it
in the teeth, and Father's clippers,
buzzing like a hive of honeybees,
letting my wavy angel wings free.

II

O

Beneath a
couple of friendly looking snakes coiling
Mercury's winged staff and frozen there in
lithograph,

this is what
the physician's message read:
Just one cellular blue disc before bed.
And do not

divagate.
Tiny as a soft sturgeon-egg,
it'll calm the heart's beast effects,
unbraid

a spongy
lung's thoracic asthmatic mess,
and knock you into an uncongested
cublike sleep.

How to resist
that summer I was ten? So I swallowed it
and every ecstatic and vile variant
that exists

to let me breathe.
Not herbal steams, hypnotism or grass,
forsaking Mother's Winstons, even my stubborness,
could relax

the sluiceways
of air I needed. A hypodermic
of fungus was the final swift cure.
Or so they

speculated.
My doctor's snout was long and square.
His needle made me kick and swear, my eyes tear.
Chastened by his

immoderateness,
I knew there was no cure: just the seasons
and their long indifference.
My body has

not escaped
this breathless state, but when its dragon-
like desolation sizzles, wild as Samson's,
I've learned to bluff

the nervous system.
As with the sun unblocking winter's snowy passage,
there follows, with the ground hog, long-awaited life
in the valley.

Three Look at One Another

Late in semi-tropic August,
    as I lay eagled in a godsend
of air whirring its
    breezy lifeline across my bed,

I spied in a village of twigs
    overhead a terrestrial thing
sweeping down the delicate boughs
    in a fiendish speed only a tree-living

shape could swing, until the limbs
    fell still again, and what had them
bristling in air arrived bedside
    all bushy and popeyed,

balanced on my window ledge
    poking his head just in, the perfect
globe of a walnut lodged in his jaw,
    when "Dash," my side-kick kitten, saw

him and blinked her sea-foam eyes
    at the thing to make it vanish,
but three were there when they opened wide,
    and it was more than heat or madness

or just plain unease
    that held us like a beast:
six eyes, so neutral yet alike
    in kingdom and surprise

that when the slim, Shaker legs
of my telephone stand plied
with photons and a clamoring
ring arrived, not even I

recognized the source of our earth-
quaked moment when it had withdrawn,
walnut trailing behind—urban
fossil of our instant, trifled and gone.

White Sheets

Alexandria, Air Force Command, 1961

Our car sped down into the earth,
rollers and cables snaking past us,
my hand pressing in on my sister's
till we landed against a buffer
and the chrome gates slid open.

The rooms were scrubbed and neat
with a yellowish glow, the men tense
with their enterprise. When he saw us,
he doffed his cap and picked me up,
twizzling his breath in my ear.
A life intransigently beautiful,
of Father's books, of Mother's china,
was left, I knew, inexplicably behind.
It was the furthest I could see
through childhood's eyes: All that we are
or could be was beating blood and salt.

The men listened in their headsets
for tremors from a country armored
as a battalion of steel, for hydrogen
eggs, big as dinosaurs', testing
beneath the earth's shield,
the flames and asbestos-suits unrevealed.
I bounced my tennis ball against a wall,
as, across a gun-metal ocean,
Khrushchev zoned the world under sickle and star.
Time, our infant sibling, was stumbling
with us through history,
surging like the white sheets
that draped the headquarters' walls,
hung for our visit, concealing
seismographic charts and bright blow-ups
of quartered hemispheres.

                                    If all of them
had loved—It burned in me—like John Rolfe
and Pocahontas wedded in my textbook
(not to speak of Reverend King
who'd yet to fall that awful spring),
unafraid of defeat, mightn't the terror
have flattened as under a tank's treads,
as in art, where inexhaustible darkness
can be cast out by tenderness?

                                    The rage,
even its complete mastery, is not enough.
This morning, long afterwards, in the gray
confusion of spring, rain streaming in the trees,
that vanished hour came back to me,
and how beyond all this, as I was
dandled upon a knee, my ears
popped from the subterranean air.

Vanessa

It was premonitions that kept us restless
the night before, visions of a gemlike lagoon
we'd push off into, the slim canoe
quivering like a magnetic needle through
narrow reefs of sedges. It was enough
to keep us fired: paddling away from
camp on marshland towards a lion's mouth of river.
At night mosquitoes, parading high-toned
outside the net, kept us captives.
Fireflies winked about the radius of our tent.
Weakened by island heat to visceral fatigue,
we slept inert as prisms in the dark night.
Tide was in when we waded into the idle current.
In a scorpion's spinal curve, it would tow us miles
into the ocean's briny green-white surf.
A dozen thirsty frogs watched beneath the oozy rim.
It seemed we could have been barbarians
plundering their defenseless world.
One foot on board, set to kick off our
bright aluminum canoe, for a split second,
I caught sight of the lagoon's woolly undercarpet
of iridescent algae. A small green ball blossomed
into a giant feeding anemone, a family
of centimeter snails nibbling its tentacle tips.
All sorts of plankton wafted about
in a rich paisley of debris that must have been home.
They were a rainbow of sea-travellers:
helmeted red-abalones, feather boas
and a lazy hermit crab sailing on a starfish.
They metamorphosed before my eyes, and quickly
as it rose, their colony blurred
beneath a wavy thicket of surfgrass.

The virgin wilderness,
its isometric shores
passing alongside us,
absorbs its conquerors

with evolutionary
good sense. Minnowlike fish,
with fiery lateral fins,
streaked beneath us.

Not an utterance rose
from the belly of marsh,
save the oars' oaken
dorsal fins. The sun arched

across the bow. Little
streams of sweat trickled
down my brow. Elsewhere
such paradisal

beauty might have sealed one's
faith in Creation,
but the world spun
with such saturnalian

power, there was only
each other to lean on.
Even the proud hairy
tarantula longed,

like Demeter, for her baby,
and the water moccasin
coiled with his marbled mate.
In my slender stern,

I felt the world swim past,
and at high noon and later,
bit by bit, our intensely flat
descent into its core.

Feet dipped overboard, straw hats tipped back, peanut butter
crackers eaten, we drifted beyond the island nucleus
in view of the Atlantic's far vanishing point. A muddy

low tide exposed whole cities of mussels
and clams cemented against the channel floor.
Sunning, they seemed short of breath, squirting spoonfuls

of sea into the air. Sweeping nearer, our silver
hull scraped against the river chasm, and we paddled off to safety.
When a meteoric pressure surged beneath us, a white-cap

rolling in our wake, I braced my sneakers into the chassis.
Air froze in my pelvis, dots of sunlight squiggled before me,
and a scaly tourmaline fin surfaced, eeling in weed-

choked circlets giant as a sea-turtle.
The saw-toothed jaw was snapping underwater
when the lizard-tail hurtled

through the surface. Almost ten feet of spine curled
across the canoe rim in a perfect teardrop
of leathery skin. Gear swept overboard as our gunnels

swamped beneath us, the mind's shutter fixing one telescopic
frame in memory: The reptile, grazing my calf in the panic,
left a trail of murky, underbelly silt before dropping

back into the sea without me.
And something in its cool, ethereal feel
reminded me, in spite of peril
of capsizing, of a moment years before
when once in the half-sleep of dawn
my sister came to my bed. I remember
it only faintly, so faintly that I have
thought, perhaps, it was only the wide net
of our dreams that wed, as children
themselves sometimes do early on to mirror
the world, and the wall our pillows abutted
the channel for our union. At moments her shape
above me was opaque as a Vanessa butterfly's
painted wings, at others I saw clear
through her to the wooded landscape beyond.
But when our tenderness had ended,
something in my impalpable recall,
unfixed or godlike, left the same
membranous residue on my adolescence
as the reptile's flailing oily tail,
and it was this isolated synapse, framing
primal images of fear and childlike
love, that steadied our canoe and kept us rowing.

Lines on Seeing the First
Color Photograph of Planet Mars

This is the day Noah might have desired
  upon the calamitous sea: a fireball of sunlight
   baking the planet with prolonged proximity;
    Mars, a giant disk of stillness,
     cradled Madonnalike by the panoramic sky.
    And so it came to Noah; in the presto of the sky,
     the flood of tom-tom clouds ceased their drumming,
     a bugle of licentious red sunlight spurged
     the earth with its zeal, and Noah's animals
      woke from congenial sleep to beget
      a colony as his patriarchal ark voyaged onward.
     Yet this faraway, velvety, bastion of repose,
      Mars, in the celestial ennui of naming,
       is christened for our God of discord,
        the blood-stained, incarnate curse of mortals.
        Beneath her gala sunlight, between her polar caps,
         across her sand dunes and at the bases of her volcanoes,
         there is only the grave drought of dust:
         everything the color of scarlet autumn,
         minus the wet and odorous, like the stinging
         rosette of a wound. No trough of a wave
       to toss us in its muscular embrace.
      No spoonfuls of icy water heaven-fallen
     across our napes. No picture frames tapping
    cheerfully against the walls. No dimpling stream.
   No athletes setting off across the lava plain.
  Not even a tortoise in its hoary carapace
could survive this rubbled disk of stone.
  That in Viking I's chromatic close-up
  I see no trifle, no bee-sweet moment of balmy spring,
only the chronic condition of a bronzing sun
unwavering as a bullet's shell of heat,
  hushes me this morning as I awake in a sun-hammered

hotel room (like Noah's goats on deck at last),
lavish with our world's caressing amenities,
and am greeted in my first yawning thought
by the perilous, topographic, Martian snapshot hung bedside.
Such a legacy is any man's terror.
We have done those things we ought not to have done
and not done those things we ought to have done,
and there is no goodness in us but the tiny song
of Noah's sparrows this April morning,
their liberty anthems ringing in our ears.

Papilloma

Naked, horizontal, marooned
    beetlelike on my spine,
a snow-white scroll of tissue unwound
    beneath me, I lie puffy-eyed

on my M.D.'s examination bed.
    The trumpet of his stethoscope
pressed to my heartbeat,
    he knocks on the doors of my chest,

pushes gently into my abdomen's
    little pillows of liver
and spleen, his hands pink as a doll's,
    probing like magnetic pincers

for the catgut's tumorous poles.
    "What have we here?" he queries
in that blue hygienic fog. We?—
    Science and I folded

like tissues before his squint-eyes,
    over us the cityscape,
a wintry, horn-shaped
    pyramid of life.

The sky, gray as stone, beams
    a glissade of snowflakes
across the longitude where I lie streaming
    with sweat, fetal and shaken,

watching the silver ornament
   of a jet glide
through its toylike descent,
   then fade

into the windowpane's bric-a-brac
   of crystals as my doctor
impales me with a needle of ice,
   excising a tiny vascular tumor,

a cauliflower of epithelial skin
   grown from the pelvis's
downward funnel, and in
   the sweet voice of an alchemist,

refusing my sober-minded
   desideratum to be heroic,
vouchsafes: *Here WE are. Benign.*
   She's a beauty, take her home!

Delirium in Castletownshend

Still panting from our journey away
from the city of bliss, the vast,
dark Atlantic spread like a gown
beneath us, he already spoke of a vague
sense of unwell-being. Crows in our wake
hours later, gravel spitting where
we parked, a tear pearled on the ridge
of his eye, his wife and I mirrored
as if in a skiff, streaking his face
with our briny wake. In the big turret-

room, the village internist, a swarthy, local boy,
noted a full span of symptoms—the neuro-
muscular network a shambles, intestines
knotted with gastric cramps, the long horizon
of his body approximating another in my mind:
Mother's twin dying inexplicably
on her side, a benign cyst at the root
of her spine, the surgeon's knife sparkling
in its place, and Mother's Lenten cry: Remember
you are dust and to dust you shall return.

Sea trout, its skin a mirage of pollution-
pink clouds, awaited us on gloomy castle Spode;
tea, toast and cornflakes at dawn; *his* night,
a chain of dry heaving and desolate, queasy sleep.
Hours skipping stones from the strand,
a clergy visit, and the lab's verdict arrived:
toxic traces routing his system, the forbidden
fruit a pint of berries, unwashed, snacked
on roadside. Amber, leopardlike patches
of sunlight covered him where he lay

thin and brittle as a sycamore stick.
A slow dementia followed, then a ghostly respite,
the estranged tongue tuned at last to speech.
He lay shiny as satin the long day,
the sudden evisceration of his mind reversing
itself, and his eyes, brine-crusted, unhooded
quartz blue irises. Sashes thrown open,
a loch breeze soughed in the leaves.
Outside, a tiny windsurfer clenched
his sail, a wave exploding beneath him.

Released at last, we ambled into the Cork hills,
nudging cattle from our paths, as behind us
the castle floated in a white shroud,
ivy ruffling the turret walls.
A fleet of sailfish skimmed the harbor.
Children tittered in the surf, the sun bronzing them
as if risen from underground into the first
glinting light of earth, where a man, like a preludium,
rolled over, feverish, weak as Adam,
to find the world luminous and waiting.

III

Caesar

Nose pressed against the glass,
Caesar sighs as morning
appointments arrive wincing
with pitiful yelps and cries that

undermine fidelity.
Coaxing them out of taxis,
away from our ginkgo's grassy
skirt, their flummoxed masters

tweak them at last and carry them
like hairy princes or barons
to our neighborhood salon
for love and caring.

Should I take him out,
my Caesar, clumsy prairie
dog to this smart set? Dare
I stroll him roundabout

our block, his snake-tail
straight in air? I do. But let him
first see his Rome a bit: his dragon-
breath fogging the view till

a big pink and blue
tongue mops the pane clear again.
Eager conquerer that he is,
he tugs me along the avenue,

his tousled hairdo one giant
cowlick crowning
a foursome of hand-me-down
paws. Despite the self-defiant

heart pounding in his chest,
they are center of his universe.
What those furry acorn eyes yearn
for is love's unharnessed zest:

Fido's blue ribbons, Ginger's
swank bubblecut, face to face
with my general's puzzled gaze—
still kin in God's house, though. Here's

proof: Let Him blow a shrill whistle,
their little tympani drumming,
the gang would yap and trail Him down.
That's love: my jeans-and-sneaker hound's.

Boy's Life

Napping pretzeled in plain old coach class,
we shifted so easily, the others and I, against

discomfort that when the smoking engine, snaking
through honey-thick sunlight ahead, braked

in its path, not one of us rose from revery,
conjuring a world ached for and awaiting us by the sea.

Our journey paused, we abandoned the dusty cars,
treading down a scarp of weeds, intrepid as Margaret,

who cut her way out of a dragon with a tiny cross,
into a field darned with thistle-blossoms.

Sunheaded and sprawled in the grass, the apparition
of our train, a silver serpent dwelling in the glare,

numbed me strangely with a knowledge imparted there:
It was a view of man apart from the world,

grumbling that the shirt of feeling we all wear,
like an angel's gilded wings,

was not the self in the glass or even real.
Somersaulting across the landscape,

I felt my heart grow colder in those moments.
Then the violet cloud tapered and was gone.

The roadman was still greasing his brakes
when we boarded, and the rails awakened

from oblivion into their harsh grip of a globe
where somewhere by the sea I would yet come to know

what I'd seen and heard. Our train gasped onward,
summer heaping its green upon us, and my legs burned

into the leather cushions, their tawny pigment seeming
more the armored plate of a tortoise, its gleam

of yellow diamonds flashing beneath me as we were carried
to a shore whose metallic surf would pitch us without sparing.

Cape Cod Elegy

Now it is only words:
that which once chastened us—
the bloodstream's genetic
war upon itself—words

and so little to see
but drowsy, sunlit History:
water at the lips silvering
through him, each capillary

a blue comatose serpent;
an untainted summer long ago,
such throat-swallowing
nakedness, inexorable as the sun, him

swimming towards me,
a hairline of copper, his torso
new-minted from the sea.
Admittedly an ancient theme:

dissolution on an endless plane
of Byzantine blue.
Enter the burning ship,
a black Lucifer through his veins.

A cruel Providence,
any youthful corpse: the devil
subverting Time. Let me recall
in the life to come the sudden

saline wave of his embrace.
And if the Lord abideth,
afterwards the moment,
a hammered bronze ornament

to guard the soul's inconstant path.
At last I believe I shall die,
though bearing this view of him: a spire
risen from a city of ash.

Ascension on Fire Island

No octopus-candelabra
  or baby Jesus adorns
the summerhouse we gather in
  to sing a hymn of forgiveness.
No churchbells bronzed overhead
  ring and set our eager mob free
when the service is said.
  Only curtains in a strong wind,

billowing like spinnakers
  upon us, seem a godly sign,
or almost so. Sharp as a new pin,
  the day begins around us,
a speckled doe nibbling
  petunias as we pray,
an excess of elementals
  piloting us forward, like Polaris,

into the gospel's verbal cathedral.
  As when Jesus appeared
to the eleven as they sat at meat
  and upbraided them with their
unbelief and hardness of heart,
  our congregation seems unknowing
at first of goodness yet to come:
  Is there a god unvexed to protect us?

What pious group wouldn't have it so!
  The floor creaks beneath us
like the hull of a ship,
  and the surf purrs in the distance,
confounding us with place,
  till a cardinal alights, twig-flexing,

anchoring us with his featherweight.
Listen for the passing stillness . . .

In the harbor a man floats
portside of his sloop, his purple
windbreaker flashing in a sunburst.
Let him be forgiven, this once,
who put him there. The family squabble,
the bruised cranium, piece by piece,
will face up to light of day.
And the body, its brief

unimmaculate youth, will be hoisted
from the water's patina of calm.
The nervous deer, the cardinal,
our perfect citizen, even invisible
bells aloft, press in upon us
with sheltering mystery,
as in the distance a throng gathers
and the yellow death-blanket unfolds.

Social Graces

Too busy or too shy to express them,
the messages of comfort to loved ones
in strange places and states that elude us,
I hunt endlessly for the right greeting
to a botanical friend, my heart stumped
by everything one never says but could:
the friendly jest—"Sorry You're Divorced,"
or the plain old truth—
"Sympathy on the Death of Your Dog."
Something with butterflies, I resolve,
but they come only in abstract. "Close-up
they're too much like bugs," the clerk admits.

I make no sharp reply, sinking deeper
into myself and the staggering precision
of FAMILY RELATIONSHIPS (each child born
into a phalanx of lives-to-be
continuing the family tree!), all the pride
of parents in sons rushing over me,
the First Communions and graduations,
the anniversary of his ordination,
or across the miles as he enters service.
Then equally the guilt, lambent everywhere,
which tears us apart to bind us together again,
from sympathizer to bereaved: "Words can't express . . ."

or from husband to wife: "I don't often tell you . . ."
The heart can hardly pick one out
in its banging desire to set things right,
each one leaving me restless as the next,
again and again, till the clerk sails on
with more breezy knowledge: "Although men die
sooner, 'Loss-of-Mother' far outsells.

And a single rose is better than a bunch.
Violets beat geraniums. Pansies whip the two."
The bestiary is just as calculated:
"Roosters come in and out of fashion.
Just now the owls and tigers are strong.

Pardon me, but animals do better than humans,
and puppies and white kittens are sure-fire."
What could I say, flushed without words, our common
needs pinpointed so, but make no excuse?
I opt for something unscented, no message but my own,
pale as any wept from the valley of tears,
but cheery, I think, testing it against my lips.
Once we've closed our eyes and the brain's murmur
has fizzled out, all that's left, really, arranged in ways
that make us feel faithful or true, are these roman letters,
so I lick my stamp, patting it kindly on the head,
and drop my effort, near weightless, at the box ahead.

Tuxedo

Millionaires at dinner
are not the Brahmins you'd think.
Long as Pinocchio's nose,
their lives are yoked by status quo:

X's nephew "pissed his million
away." *She* saved the condo though.
Even bitter as she is,
her breasts shiver like an aspic

in her velvet bodice.
Thin blood, thin air:
Y's nosebleed leaves a lipstick-
red trail throughout the affair.

Not even her sable boa gets a stare.
After espresso six spiral-haired
ladies, coquettish as girls,
"go pee" in tandem. Pearly

white, the powder room sees
their lives pass through its mirrors,
hears them praise their
hostess and her lamb. A fleet

of hearses, the tycoons
idle in the china-blue ballroom,
their petroleum-black lapels glossy
as new-buffed fenders. Exhaust

snakes from their awful Havana
cigars, setting the wives sneezing
on return in a heliostream
of taffeta and organza.

"God bless us!" they protest
at the smog. And He does.
For perfect as their chromosomes,
their destiny is Embassy Row,

where their homes have mighty
wings with electric eyes and tiny
twinbeds unwrapped like mints
for them to sleep in, each in each.

Lost in Venice

"Which is better—the world or seclusion? . . . so much is certain—either life entails courage or it ceases to be life." E.M. FORSTER

Across the Continent the operator
crackled on the line. Three rings and a faint
    voice, bolted from sleep and snorting:
My card. Did it reach you? Its grainy
    intaglio scene etched in mind,
        posted from Paris, escaping delays—
        the view: a gothic palace riding
    the canal, his flat designated

    by eight blacked-out windows
in the crown. *Can you come?*
    his saintly query. The train inched
through the alps, my neighbor's plump
    poodle asleep between us.
        Our bellies filled with lunch,
        our heads shook on their rests,
        and the track bore us sunward . . .

    Glints of Adriatic blue and the cars
lifted onto a viaduct arching
    across a spit of land and sparked
to a halt on the choppy canal.
    These things hold through weariness:
        my host's white silk pullover,
        his tanned arms waving in the air
        (*Here we are!*), the slow, autumnal

cumulus plumped overhead,
mirrored in his cataracted eyes.
        Duffel bag shouldered, we headed
for home, my eyes tracing the liquefied
        city, its parquet of streets dowsed
            clean and interlaced with a spate
                of churchbells. A treasure heap of houses,
            as Ruskin declared, partly gold, maybe,

            partly opal and mother-of-pearl.
Nights and days blur
        under a roof with sparrows,
entered from an atrium
        of stone steps, pillows nearly,
            draped in ivy and rippling three
                floors high into the palace eaves
            where his rooms were situated,

            where we lingered at sunset with drinks
in the library beneath a vaulted
        cavernous ceiling of gesso washes
and ornate stuccos to recount each
        day's aquatinted discoveries,
            the canal's rosy surfaces peeking
                in upon us. Was this where James slept,
            having penned in one infectious

            sitting "The Aspern Papers," a story
smoking with thwarted will? So
        palace legend had it. Charmed by the notion,
if doubtful, my host
        lifted his tumbler, toasting the rooms
            and his seclusion there. A halo
                of white hair, turbanlike, illumined
            his head in a vertical ray,

and in the faint sunbeamed shaft,
this unmeaning apparition passed:
    At a gallery on the lagoon that day,
near the foot of Proust's double chain
    of marble cliffs, houses really,
        angling in sunlight, I'd paused
           before a massive canvas
      of the shepherd boy, David, caught

    with his sling in action.
The Philistine giant loomed
    above him, yet David, the beloved one,
steadied his aim for slaying.
    It drugged me for a moment—
        his unpitying task—when a
           sudden knowledge floated
      into the gallery like a dove

    wobbling high against the domed sky-
lights, lost in the honeycomb
    of endless rooms.
It was not Goliath's
    spasmodic growl that spoke to me,
        or even David's cautious approach,
           but a kind of rudderless knowing
      that sequined in his eye, as if we

    all uneasily inherit
his path: the humble origin,
    the unblinking test of faith,
the final annointed killing.
    A bitter fountain to drink from,
        though rejuvenating . . . My host would live
           on a year, and young David
      reign half a century as King. Had one

of us strayed those long illusory
days lost in Venice,
what could have happened? And the legacy?—
for that one dreamy scotchlit moment, we
were inured to it. In the darkening
night, black gondolas skimmed beneath us,
and a tenor's silver crescendo touched
the air like a shepherd boy's sweet harping.

(DAVID KALSTONE, 1932–1986)

The Zoo Wheel of Knowledge

for Christopher Bram and Draper Shreeve

The difficulty to see at the end of day:
She's sprinkling flour in the bronze light,
he's spooning apricots into our infant,
and Star, marauder of the yards and alleys,

is sleeping in the next room, wriggling
on his haunches, ears flapping, his red eyes
in a dream rushing away with their catch,
his tongue a spear in our hearts.

How strange to hear in the fading sun
the little girls from Sacred Heart scream
and rush against each other when the lions
in the park let go their convulsive roar,

awakening in us, as with the addict,
a spasmlike hunger to please the beast.
So we set off, all of us, guiding our stroller,
the baby's head floating before us as through

the dark, arctic tanks where the bears
glide, monsterlike yet sultry,
their eyes opening, brown as mother's,
at the viewing window, their phosphorescent

trunks so white and godlike
a neighbor's sons, one night, scaled the wall
to dive and kick among them.
Pity the poor beasts, weary, gazing upward—

save the congress of bats asleep in its cave—
as for the stars that mirror them
in constellation: Pavo, the peacock;
tough skinned Leo; the golden fleeced ram;

Aquila, the eagle; even little Lepus, the hare,
whom all the children pet at the petting station.
Whatever happens to them, mishap or fortune,
is as well for us with downy fur on our spines.

Each child freezes them in Kodak—
above us the ape's lips are cracked and bleeding,
his pink tits pumped up from swinging
in the canopy—and therefore ourselves

in rendezvous this first light of evening,
as at a pageant or crazy fantasia
of the unconscious where we all collect
eventually, even Star and the souls

of the boys found in the polar tank.
All of us writhing in a kind of heroic
remembering of what our natures are—
the unspeakable resemblance, the distant

mother-tongue—though the cage-bars
frame us apart. The gold eyes
look outward, near bodiless in the dim light,
as in that halcyon moment when bison, herding,

lift their flecked heads at once toward
the hills, knowing they'll take possession.
Oh Lord, make us sure as the beasts
who drink from the pond, their shaggy manes

dappled with air; who see those that flee
from them, yet wait and breathe accustomed
to the night; and who listen tirelessly
for grasses to blow on the plain again.

HENRI COLE was born in Fukuoka, Japan in 1956. He grew up in Virginia and was graduated by the College of William and Mary. He holds graduate degrees from the University of Wisconsin and Columbia University and is the recipient of fellowships from the Ingram Merrill Foundation and the New York Foundation for the Arts. His poems have been published in *Antaeus, The Atlantic Monthly, The Nation, The New Yorker, The Paris Review, The Yale Review* and *Poetry,* and his first full-length collection, *The Marble Queen,* was published in 1986. He lives in New York City and is the Amy Lowell Poetry Travelling Scholar for 1989–90.

A NOTE ON THE TYPE

The text of this book has been set on the Linotype in a typeface called Baskerville. It is a facsimile reproduction of types cast from molds made for John Baskerville (1706–1775) from his designs. The punches for the revived Linotype Baskerville were cut under the supervision of the English printer George W. Jones. John Baskerville's original face was one of the forerunners of the type-style known as "modern face" to printers: a "modern" of the period A.D. 1800.

Composition by
Heritage Printers, Inc., Charlotte, North Carolina.
Printed and bound by
Halliday Lithographers, Inc., West Hanover, Massachusetts
Designed by Harry Ford.